Learn 'n' Enjoy

FLOWERS

Published By
DISCOVERY PUBLISHING HOUSE PVT. LTD.

**4383/4 - A, ANSARI ROAD, DARYA GANJ,
NEW DELHI - 110002 (INDIA)
TEL : +91-11-23279245 / 43596064 / 43596065
FAX : +91-11-23253475
E-MAIL : parul.wasan@gmail.com
info@discoverykidz.in
WEB :- www.discoverykidz.in**

AF730037

ROSE

SUNFLOWER

HIBISCUS

MARIGOLD

HYACINTH

DAHLIA

DAISY

POPPY

LOTUS

WATERLILY

TULIP

PERIWINKLE

PANSY

MORNING GLORY

CANNA